The Contender

and Related Readings

McDougal Littell
A HOUGHTON MIFFLIN COMPANY

Evanston, Illinois • Boston • Dallas

Links to *The Language of Literature*

If you are using *The Contender* in conjunction with *The Language of Literature,* please note that thematic connections can be easily made between the novel and the following units:

- Grade 8, Unit 3: Battle for Control
- Grade 8, Unit 5: Personal Discoveries
- Grade 7, Unit 3: Stepping Forward

Acknowledgments

Pages 8–9: Excerpt from "Forum: Robert Lipsyte on Kids/Sports/Books," from *Children's Literature in Education*, vol. 11, no. 1, Spring 1980. Reprinted by permission of Plenum Publishing Corporation.

Page 10: Excerpt from "Up the Stairs Alone: Robert Lipsyte on Writing for Young Adults" by Sari Feldman, from *Top of the News*, vol. 39, no. 2, Winter 1983. Copyright © 1983 by the American Library Association. Reprinted with permission of the American Library Association.

Pages 10–11: Excerpt from book review by Susan O'Neal in *School Library Journal*, November 1967. Copyright © by Cahners Publishing Company, a division of Reed Elsevier Inc. Reprinted with permission from School Library Journal.

Page 11: Excerpt from book review by Nat Hentoff in *The New York Times Book Review*, November 12, 1967. Copyright © 1967 by The New York Times Company. Reprinted by permission of The New York Times.

ISBN 0-395-83359-0

34567—MAL—03 02 01

Table of Contents

Parts of the SourceBook

- • Table of Contents
- • Overview Chart
- • Summaries of the Literature
- • Customizing Instruction

Into the Literature
CREATING CONTEXT

- • **Cultural/Historical/Author Background**
- • **Critic's Corner** Excerpts from literary criticism about *The Contender*
- • **Literary Concepts**
- • **Motivating Activities**

Through the Literature
DEVELOPING
UNDERSTANDING

- • **Discussion Starters** Questions for the class to respond to orally after reading each section, including a Literary Concept question and a Writing Prompt
- (FYI) **FYI Pages for Students** Reproducible masters that offer students background, vocabulary help, and connections to the modern world as they read the literature
- (FYI) **Glossary** Reproducible glossary of difficult words from each section of *The Contender*
- • **Strategic Reading worksheets** Reproducible masters to help students keep track of the plot as they read (Literal and inferential reading)
- • **Literary Concept worksheets** Reproducible masters to help students understand the use of literary elements (Critical reading)
- • **Vocabulary worksheet** Reproducible master to help students learn essential vocabulary used in the novel

Beyond the Literature
SYNTHESIZING
IDEAS

- • **Culminating Writing Assignments** Exploratory, research, and literary analysis topics for writing, covering both the main work and the related readings
- • **Multimodal Activities** Suggestions for short-term projects; some are cross-curricular.
- • **Cross-Curricular Projects** Suggestions for long-term, cross-curricular, cooperative learning projects
- • **Suggestions for Assessment**
- • **Test, Answer Key** Essay and short-answer test on *The Contender* and additional selections, and answer key
- • **Additional Resources** Additional readings for students (coded by difficulty level) and teachers, as well as bibliographic information about commercially available technology

Overview Chart

Literature Connections	SourceBook	Reproducible Pages
The Contender	Customizing Instruction, p. 5 Creating Context, pp. 6–9 Critic's Corner, pp. 10–11 Literary Concepts, pp. 12–14 Motivating Activities, p. 15	**FYI, p. 24** **Glossary, p. 30** **Vocabulary, p. 36**
The Contender Section 1, pp. 3–69	Discussion Starters, p. 16	**FYI, p. 25** **Glossary, p. 30** **Strategic Reading 1, p. 31**
The Contender Section 2, pp. 70–157	Discussion Starters, p. 17	**FYI, p. 26** **Glossary, p. 30** **Strategic Reading 2, p. 32** **Literary Concept 1–3, pp. 33–35**
"The Seventh Round," p. 163	Discussion Starters, p. 18	
"Fury," pp. 164–191	Discussion Starters, p. 18	
from *The Story of My Life*, pp. 192–200	Discussion Starters, p. 19	**FYI, p. 27**
"A Crown of Wild Olive," pp. 201–226	Discussion Starters, p. 20	**FYI, p. 28**
"The Rights to the Streets of Memphis," pp. 227–232	Discussion Starters, p. 21	
"Joan Benoit: 1984 U.S. Olympic Gold Medalist," pp. 233–234	Discussion Starters, p. 21	
"Muhammad Ali," pp. 235–244	Discussion Starters, p. 22	**FYI, p. 29**
"To the Field Goal Kicker in a Slump," p. 245	Discussion Starters, p. 22	
	Culminating Writing Assignments, p. 37* Multimodal Activities, pp. 38–39 Cross-Curricular Projects, pp. 40–41 Suggestions for Assessment, p. 42 Test, Answer Key, pp. 43–46 Additional Resources, pp. 47–49	

*Additional writing support for students can be found in **Writing Coach.**

The Contender
by Robert Lipsyte

Alfred Brooks is an African-American youth whose life is going nowhere. Living in Harlem during the 1960s, when the civil rights movement is beginning to open doors for African Americans, Alfred has dropped out of high school. He works a menial job in a grocery store and spends much of his time watching movies. Estranged from his best friend and targeted by a gang of thugs, he desperately wants to turn his life around. One night, he wanders into a gym and meets Vito Donatelli, a manager deeply concerned for the fighters he trains. Alfred puts himself through the rigor and discipline of training, building muscle and endurance and developing boxing skills. All the while, one question nags at him—whether he has the heart of a contender. One way to find out is to step into the ring against a brutal ex-Marine and stand up to the vicious battering of his fists.

RELATED READINGS

The Seventh Round
by James Merrill

As the crowd at ringside screams for blood, the speaker of this poem tries to withstand a barrage of blows.

Fury
by T. Ernesto Bethancourt

In this short story, an uncle tries to help his wayward nephew get the discipline he needs to succeed in the ring and in life.

from ***The Story of My Life***
by Helen Keller

This excerpt describes the difference a teacher can make.

A Crown of Wild Olive
by Rosemary Sutcliff

Two athletes from different ways of life discover the meaning of friendship as they compete against each other in the ancient Olympic games.

The Rights to the Streets of Memphis
by Richard Wright

In this excerpt from his autobiography, Richard Wright recalls a lesson in courage that his mother taught him.

Joan Benoit: 1984 U.S. Olympic Marathon Gold Medalist
by Rina Ferrarelli

The speaker of this poem admires the poise, control, and "inner rhythm" of a remarkable runner in the heat of competition.

Muhammad Ali
by Bill Littlefield

This biography focuses on the legendary boxer whose private struggles were as riveting as his battles in the ring.

To the Field Goal Kicker in a Slump
by Linda Pastan

This poem is about the frustrations of a place-kicker who is not getting the job done.

Customizing Instruction

Less Proficient Readers

- To prepare students for reading the novel, preview the novel's setting and its main character. Note that the story takes place in Harlem, a largely African-American district in New York City, in the 1960s. Discuss what Harlem was like in the 1960s, using the information provided in **Creating Context,** page 6. Tell students that the main character is African American and is a recent high-school dropout.

- If necessary, read the novel aloud to students or have them take turns reading it aloud in small groups. Make sure that students understand the relationships that the writer establishes in Chapter 1, especially the one between Alfred and his estranged friend James. Ask students to summarize what happens in each chapter after reading it. Encourage students to focus on how Alfred changes as the novel progresses.

- To help with literal comprehension, have students use the **Strategic Reading 1–2** worksheets, pages 31–32, as they read.

- Reproduce the Glossary (page 30) for students to use as they read.

Students Acquiring English

- To help students gain an appreciation of the setting of the novel, show photographs of Harlem, and help them locate Harlem on a map of New York City.

- If students have little knowledge of boxing, bring a few boxing books to class and have students look at the photographs. To provide them with some basic information about boxing, preview the **FYI** page 24. You might also show one of the boxing videotapes listed in the **Additional Resources** on page 49.

- Preview the definition and connotations of key vocabulary words, such as *champion* and *contender.*

- Point out that much of the dialogue in the novel is in an African-American dialect and discuss a few examples. You might pair native speakers with students acquiring English and have them take turns reading passages of dialogue aloud.

- If appropriate, use the suggestions for less proficient readers.

Gifted and Talented Students

- Have students begin a word web for the word *contender,* jotting down all the associations they have with the word. As they read the novel, suggest that they add to their word web as they gain new insights into the meaning of the word.

- Share one or more of the reviews in the Critic's Corner with students and suggest that they look for evidence in the novel that supports or disproves the critic's opinion.

- Challenge students to give each chapter a title after reading it. At the end, students might list all the titles in order to see whether they create a summary of the plot of the novel.

- Have students imagine experiences that Alfred and James share before and after the events described in the novel. Have small groups plan and perform a skit based on one of these experiences.

Into the Literature

The Contender

Robert Lipsyte wrote *The Contender*, his first novel for young adults, in the mid-1960s while he was a sports writer for the New York Times. In writing the novel, Lipsyte drew upon his experience in covering professional boxing, especially Muhammad Ali's career. The inspiration for the novel came from Lipsyte's meeting with an aging boxing manager who spoke about judging young boys as possible contenders. Before writing *The Contender*, Lipsyte had worked closely with African-American comedian and civil rights leader Dick Gregory on an autobiography. Because of this experience, Lipsyte thought he could create a central character who was black, even though Lipsyte himself is white.

The Contender became a best-selling, award-winning novel, but critical assessment of it was mixed. Some critics praised the novel's realism, while others viewed the portrayal of both black and white characters as overly simplistic. But at the time *The Contender* was written, few young adult novels featured African Americans as main characters. And very few dealt with such problems as drug abuse, crime, and poverty.

Harlem in the 1960's

Harlem is a district of New York City that covers a large part of northern Manhattan Island. In the early 1900s, Harlem became established as a largely African-American residential area. By the 1960s, Harlem had become an overcrowded, impoverished community. Most residents lived in rundown apartment buildings, and the community's unemployment and crime rates ran high.

In the 1960s black nationalists, who sought to build the political and economic strength of African Americans, organized in Harlem, led by the controversial Muslim leader Malcolm X. While leaders in the civil rights movement sought integration, the black nationalists wanted to create a separate black nation within the United States. The 1960s saw Harlem erupt in riots in which blacks protested exploitation by white merchants as well as poor living conditions.

The World of Boxing

Though a brutal sport, boxing has been popular in the United States, especially from the 1920s to the 1940s. In the early years of this century, waves of immigrants turned to boxing as a path to fame and riches in America. Successive decades saw Irish, Jewish, and Italian Americans rise to the top in professional boxing. African Americans have also been prominent in the sport, including such champions as Jack Johnson, Joe Louis, and Muhammad Ali. Most professional boxers have come from impoverished backgrounds. With little education and limited job opportunities, boxers have sought a chance to gain status and wealth, even at the risk of serious injury and possibly even death. But while the few at the top of the boxing world have become rich, most of the rest have not. And for the most part, boxing has had a seamy reputation because of the involvement of organized crime and unscrupulous promoters.

Robert Lipsyte's Life

Although his writing career has focused on the world of sports, Robert Lipsyte had little early experience as an actual player. Born in New York City in 1938, he grew up in a largely Jewish neighborhood. His father was a principal and his mother a teacher. Overweight as a child, Lipsyte spent much of his time reading. At the age of fourteen, however, he trimmed down and suddenly became active in sports. He later described this transformation in his novel *One Fat Summer,* in which an overweight teenager slims down during a summer of cutting lawns.

After graduating in 1957 from Columbia University, Lipsyte took a job as a copy boy in the sports department of the *New York Times.* He went on to become a sports reporter and columnist for the newspaper. In 1964 Lipsyte began covering the sport of boxing, and for more than three years, he followed the career of Muhammad Ali, then the heavyweight champion. Considering Ali "far and away the most interesting character" in the sports world, Lipsyte later wrote a biography of him entitled *Free to Be Muhammad Ali.* Unlike many sports biographers for young readers, Lipsyte writes unsentimental profiles of sports figures, portraying them as complex people with both strengths and weaknesses.

Although he received national acclaim for his sports columns, Lipsyte left the *New York Times* in 1971 to devote more time to writing, both fiction and nonfiction. For the next eleven years, he wrote books, taught college journalism, and even composed jokes for a television show. Then in 1982 he became a TV correspondent and talk-show host, taking an eight-year break from writing. But his career turned full circle. In 1991 he published *The Brave,* the sequel to *The Contender,* and returned to the *New York Times* to write a weekly sports column.

In writing for young adults, Lipsyte strives to put sports in proper perspective. "If we write more truthfully about sports, perhaps we can encourage kids to relax and have fun with each other—to challenge themselves for the pleasure of it, without self-doubt and without fear."

Lipsyte on Lipsyte

On his early years—

"I grew up in Rego Park, in Queens, then a neighborhood of attached houses, six-story apartment buildings, and many vacant jungly lots. We played guns in the lots, Chinese handball against the brick sides of buildings, and just enough stickball in the streets and schoolyard to qualify, years later in midtown bars, as true natives. There was no great sporting tradition in the neighborhood, few organized sports of any kind, and only one sports temple, the West Side Tennis Club in adjacent Forest Hills, which accepted neither Negroes, of whom we saw few, nor Jews, which most of us were."

FROM *SPORTSWORLD: AN AMERICAN DREAMLAND* BY ROBERT LIPSYTE

On his entry into sportswriting—

In 1957, a few days after graduation from Columbia [University], I answered a classified ad for a copy boy at *The Times*. I wanted a summer job to pay my way out to graduate school in California, but the personnel interviewer assumed I was seeking a career foothold. . . .

The job was at night, from 7 to 3, and it was in the sports department, filling paste-pots, sharpening pencils and fetching coffee for the night sports copy desk. . . .

For a son of the so-called silent generation, too independent to work for a corporation yet lacking a Beat poet's confidence, journalism was a compromise that seemed like a calling. By the end of that first paste-pot summer I knew I would stay. It probably came down to something as romantic as the tremor in my bowels each night when the great machines in the subbasement roared to life with the start of the press run. I felt emotionally, intellectually, viscerally part of something big and good and even a little daring. I would be a Newslinger, too.

FROM *SPORTSWORLD: AN AMERICAN DREAMLAND* BY ROBERT LIPSYTE

On his ideas about kids and sports—

Sports is, or should be, just one of the things people do—an integral part of life, but only one aspect of it. Sports is a good experience. It's fun. It ought to be inexpensive and accessible to everybody. Kids should go out and play, test and extend their bodies, feel good about what they can achieve on their own or with a team. And children's books about sports should encourage that approach.

Instead, adults try to make sports into a metaphor—a preparation for life. We endow sports with mystical qualities that don't exist and raise unreal expectations about what it can do. At the same time, by making sports into a metaphor, we devalue it for itself. It's no wonder that the kids who read sports books are confused by them. . . .

What the books don't say is that in our society, sports is a negative experience for most boys and almost all girls. Soon after they start school, at an age when they have no other standards on which to judge themselves, we force children to judge each other on their bodies, which is the thing that everyone's most scared about. They're required to define themselves on the basis of competitive physical ability. . . .

I'd like to see sports books for children that would take away some of the pressures they feel and defuse the sense of competition and rejection. To do this, I think the books must acknowledge children's real fears about sports.

The first, perhaps ultimate, fear is of being ridiculed—the fear that everyone's going to laugh at you because you're not good. . . .

A second fear is the fear of getting hurt. . . .

A third fear that kids have about sports is of disappointing their parents. . . .

Finally, there's the basic, overall fear of not measuring up in sports—not being man enough, or woman enough. This may be the most meaningless definition of being a worthy person in our society.

FROM "FORUM: ROBERT LIPSYTE ON KIDS/SPORTS/BOOKS"
CHILDREN'S LITERATURE IN EDUCATION, VOL. 11, NO. 1 (SPRING), 1980

On his bout with cancer in 1978—

Like most people, we regarded cancer as one of the most dread words in the language: if not a death sentence, we thought, at least it meant the end of a normal, productive life. We knew very little about cancer, but we learned quickly. After surgery, I underwent two years of chemotherapy. I was sick for a day or two after each treatment, and I lost some strength and some hair, but we were amazed at how normally my life continued: I wrote, I traveled, I swam and ran and played tennis. After the treatments were over, my strength and my hair returned. There was no evidence of cancer. I was happy to be alive, to be enjoying my family, to be writing.

FROM *SOMETHING ABOUT THE AUTHOR,* VOLUME 68, 1992

Critic's Corner

SARI FELDMAN

Feldman, Sari. "Up the Stairs Alone: Robert Lipsyte on Writing for Young Adults." *Top of the News,* Vol. 39, No. 2, Winter, 1983, pp. 198–202.

The Contender may seem quite sentimental, but in 1967 the realities of urban life were just beginning to be revealed, particularly to teenagers. The optimism of *The Contender* reflects the social vision of the "Great Society," a vision that remains unrealized. Today the well-meaning white adults of the novel are seen in a more sophisticated light and could be viewed as paternalistic or inadvertently exploiting impoverished neighborhoods and impressionable youth. It is the themes of *The Contender* and the vivid sports action that keep the book pertinent to a 1980 audience. "I think today *The Contender* is a girl gymnast in a well-to-do suburban high school," Lipsyte acknowledged.

The Contender owes its inspiration to a chance meeting with an aging boxing manager in Las Vegas. "He was old, he was going blind, kind of shuffling through the scene and he began to reminisce and he talked about this gym that he had once owned that was up three flights of stairs on the Lower East Side," Lipsyte recalled. "He used to sit at the top of those stairs listening to boys come up the steps and he could judge whether or not they would ever be contenders. He could tell because he was waiting for the boy who came up alone, one set of footsteps, a boy who came at night and a boy who came up scared, the footsteps kind of scurrying, or at least not confident. That boy was going to conquer his fear because he was so desperate to become somebody."

This image stayed in Lipsyte's mind and started him thinking about the word *contender* in a very symbolic way. What are the moments in life that are equivalent to "going up the stairs"? His ruminations led to the development of the Brooks character.

Today a white author might not risk creating a central black character. "In retrospect," Lipsyte revealed, "I'm appalled at my arrogance that I could have, I'm not so sure I should have." At that time Lipsyte had just come out of an intensive nine months with Dick Gregory, getting an exposure to black culture and gaining confidence to realistically relate to and write about the black experience. They co-authored Gregory's autobiography of his early years and personal struggles. "Just from working on [the autobiography], talking to him (Gregory), meeting his friends, listening to reminiscences, talking about the sense of being black, I felt that maybe I could present a story in a reportorial way."

SUSAN O'NEAL

O'Neal, Susan. Review of "The Contender." *School Library Journal,* Vol. 14, No. 3, November, 1967, p. 78

Admirably, the author tries to portray Alfred's world through the boy's own eyes, and like *Durango Street,* in his own language, but too often Mr. Lipsyte oversimplifies. For instance, white characters are paragons of interest and devotion; black nationalist ideas invariably come from the mouths of addicts and thugs, thus constituting a kind of guilt by association. Most important, only one way of responding to complicated problems is made to appear valid. Alfred's decision to compete by conventional methods is considered by the author to be the only proper action and is pitted against the attitude of Alfred's unsuccessful friends that, in any case, "Whitey" won't let you make it in his world. The implication, whether intended or not, is that Alfred's friends are the chief cause of their own trouble. Such assignment of blame, however, makes the very real pressures that provoke these feelings in the ghetto teen-agers seem trivial. As a sports story, this is a superior, engrossing, insider's book; but as social commentary on problems in a Negro ghetto, it is a superficial, outsider's book which doesn't increase real understanding. But the book is worth trying out to see how the Alfreds react.

NAT HENTOFF

Hentoff, Nat. Review of "The Contender." *The New York Times Book Review,* November 12, 1967, p. 42.

On this homiletic level, the material is so neatly and obviously manipulated that virtue will have to be its own reward because *The Contender* —as a whole—fails as believable fiction. In several of its parts, however, didacticism recedes, and lo, there is life! In particular, whenever Lipsyte writes about boxing itself he indicates how intensely evocative he can be and he moves the reader beyond maxims into participation.

Lipsyte is most convincing in his unfolding of the inner transformation of a boy gone slack into a boxer gradually responding to different and compelling rhythms as he is driven by self-stretching imperatives, as emotional as they are physical. Within his factitious outer framework Lipsyte occasionally lets his main character become palpable.

It is when he leaves the gym and the ring that Lipsyte is too often content to map the road to salvation, rather than explore much more deeply the present ghetto terrain of his dropout. Can the lessons in more-than-survival that are learned in the ring be as easily applied as *The Contender* promises in neighborhoods where the rules of the game and the odds are set by distant outside societal forces? If the Horatio Alger approach is to be at all relevant in a work of fiction set in the ghetto, it needs to be considerably updated and treated with much less naiveté than here.

JOHN S. SIMMONS

Simmons, John S. "Lipsyte's 'Contender': Another Look at the Junior Novel." *Elementary English,* Vol. XLIX, No. 1, January, 1972, pp. 116–119.

As an inducement to the inveterate symbol hunters in the teaching gentry, *The Contender* provides a couple of fairly obvious ones. Comprehending the significance of the continued use of the cave and the stairs in the novel will not constitute an overly frustrating task for large numbers of early adolescent readers. Their placing in the novel and the care taken with their description make them relatively easy to place in clear symbolic perspective.

Literary Concept
THEME

The idea of transformation plays a major role in many of Lipsyte's young adult novels. Essentially a before-and-after novel, *The Contender* focuses on the positive changes in a teenage boy who finds direction in his life through the sport of boxing. Criticized by some reviewers for being overly moralistic and simplistic, *The Contender* conveys a number of messages to young people. Below are statements of some of the themes that run through the novel:

- It's the effort and struggle that make a person, not winning or success.
- It takes courage, discipline, hard work, and inner strength to change one's life.
- It's worse to quit something you want to achieve than never to begin at all.
- A contender in any field works hard to climb as far as possible, knowing he or she may not reach the top.
- To achieve something worthwhile, you must learn to face and control your fears.
- Each person must try to find out what he or she is capable of achieving.
- Young people need friends and/or role models to help and guide them.
- Inner strength is more important than physical ability.
- A good coach has the trainee's best interest at heart.

Presentation Suggestions You might remind students that a **theme** of a literary work is a message that the writer shares with the reader. The message may be a lesson about life or about people and their actions. A literary work may convey several themes, and different readers may discover different themes in the same work. To explore the themes in *The Contender*, you might have students complete the **Literary Concept 1** worksheet, on page 33, either while they read the novel or after they have finished reading. Students might use their worksheets as a springboard for a class discussion on the major themes of the novel.

Literary Concept
CHARACTERIZATION

The Contender charts the evolution of Alfred Brooks from a drifting, directionless youth with low self-esteem to a purposeful, confident young man. In the beginning of the novel, Alfred has recently dropped out of high school and has gotten a menial job in a grocery store. Even though he lacks a sense of purpose, Alfred, unlike some of his peers, has not yet descended into a life of drug abuse and crime. The sport of boxing changes Alfred, giving him an opportunity to come under the guidance of wise adults and to acquire self-discipline. As he develops physically, he gains confidence, gradually realizing that the challenges he has met in learning how to box enable him to meet any other challenges in life. Thus, boxing becomes a positive influence not because it offers a way out of poverty, but because it teaches Alfred the value of hard work and determination. By the end of the novel, Alfred has changed not only physically but also psychologically. He has matured and has found a new direction in life, planning to complete his education and to work in a neighborhood recreation center for youth. Moreover, he now has the strength to rescue his friend James, tending his physical wounds and supporting him on his way to the hospital and to a drug-free future.

Many of the other characters in the novel might be divided into those who are positive influences on Alfred and those who are negative influences. The positive influences include Aunt Pearl, Mr. Donatelli, Lou Epstein, Henry, and Spoon. The negative influences include Major and his followers. But other than Alfred, most of the other characters are static and not fully developed.

Presentation Suggestions Remind students that **characterization** refers to the techniques a writer uses to bring characters to life. There are four basic methods of characterization: 1) physically describing the character; 2) presenting the character's thoughts, speech, and actions; 3) showing how others respond to the character; and 4) directly commenting on the character's nature.

Advise students to look for the methods Lipsyte uses to make such characters as Alfred, Aunt Pearl, Major, Donatelli, James, and Spoon come alive in their imaginations. Have them complete the **Literary Concept 2** worksheet, on page 34, as or after they read the novel. Students will discover that the author uses the first three methods of characterization. Challenge students to explain why Lipsyte chose not to use the fourth method.

Literary Concept
CONFLICT

Athletic contests by their very nature involve **conflict,** a struggle between two opposing forces, and the title of Lipsyte's novel, *The Contender*, refers to a boxer struggling to reach a goal. In his search to find and maintain a direction in his life, Alfred Brooks faces conflict on every front: within himself, against other characters, and against forces in society. Although he has a loving home, Alfred lacks confidence, his peers want to lead him into a life of drugs and crime, and he is subjected to the opposing values of black militancy and Christianity. In developing the physical strength to meet challengers within the ring, Alfred gains the inner strength to meet challenges outside it.

Presentation Suggestions Remind students that a **conflict** is a struggle between opposing forces and that it is the basis of a story's plot. An **external conflict** pits a character against nature, society, or another character. An **internal conflict** involves opposing forces within a character. You may use the **Literary Concept 3** worksheet, on page 35, to help students explore conflict as or after they read the novel.

Motivating Activities

1. **Concept Web** Ask students to work independently or in small groups to create a word web that lists what they know about boxing and the associations they have with this sport. To model this activity for students, draw on the chalkboard a web that list the details shown below.

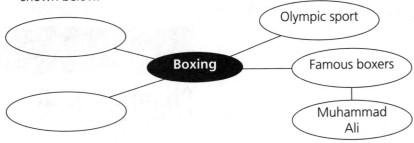

If students know little about boxing, you might show them one of the boxing videotapes listed in the **Additional Resources** on page 49.

2. **Linking to Today: Sports as a Way Up** For decades, many members of disadvantaged groups in the United States have viewed sports as a means for their children to rise up and out of poverty. Ask students to name sports figures who came from impoverished backgrounds. List each name and the sport each plays or played on the chalkboard. Challenge students to design a poster or a trading card that features one of the sports figures listed. Then discuss with students the pros and cons of regarding sports as an avenue to a better life.

3. **Tapping Prior Knowledge: Playing Sports** Invite students to share some of their experiences while playing sports or participating in any other challenging activity. Have a class discussion in which students explore questions like the following: What sport do you most enjoy playing, and why? What qualities did you develop by participating in sports? How important do you think sports are in the lives of many young people? What traits do you especially admire in the coaches and trainers you have met?

4. **QuickWrites** Have students jot down in their notebooks their ideas about social problems such as poverty, quitting school, and drug abuse. Pose questions like the following for students to explore:

   • Why do you think some students decide to drop out of high school?

   • What kinds of jobs are available for high school dropouts?

   • Why do you think some youths get involved with drugs?

   • What opportunities for self-improvement are available for high school dropouts in poverty-stricken communities?

   Suggest that students refer to their notes after reading the novel to assess how their thinking about these social problems might have developed.

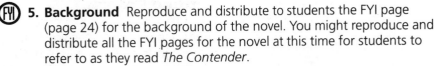

5. **Background** Reproduce and distribute to students the FYI page (page 24) for the background of the novel. You might reproduce and distribute all the FYI pages for the novel at this time for students to refer to as they read *The Contender*.

BEFORE READING

You might want to distribute

 p. 25, Glossary, p. 30

• *Strategic Reading 1, p. 31*

The Contender

Chapters 1—9

AFTER READING

Discussion Starters

1. What words would you use to describe your impressions of Alfred at the end of Chapter 9?

2. What do you predict might happen to Alfred as he trains under Mr. Donatelli?

3. How would you describe Alfred's physical and mental changes by the end of Chapter 9?

4. Why do you think Alfred is able to stand up to Major when he threatens to slash his face?

CONSIDER

✓ his home life, his job, and his prospects for the future

✓ his self-image

✓ the influence of Mr. Donatelli, Henry, and the others at the gym

✓ the presence of Major and his gang in the neighborhood

5. What do you think is the main reason why Alfred is drawn to boxing?

6. **Literary Concept: Theme** What do you think Mr. Donatelli means by the statement, "It's the climbing that makes the man"? Explain whether or not you agree with him.

7. **Making Connections** Do you think that disadvantaged youth today still regard sports as a way to be "somebody"? Give reasons to support your opinion.

Writing Prompt

Think about a time when you made an important change in your life. Write a **journal entry** in which you describe the change, why you wanted to make it, and what you did to make it happen.

SECTION 2

Chapters 10–20

AFTER READING

Discussion Starters

1. What thoughts do you have after finishing this story? Write them in your notebook.
2. What do you predict will happen to Alfred's friend James, and why?
3. Consider the factors that bring about Alfred's transformation. Which one of these factors do you consider most important, and why?
4. Imagine that Mr. Donatelli refuses to allow Alfred to fight Elston Hubbard. What effect do you think this decision would have had on Alfred's future?
5. How would you evaluate Mr. Donatelli as a trainer of boxers?

> ### CONSIDER
>
> ✓ the qualities you admire in a coach or a trainer
>
> ✓ his advice to Alfred at their first meeting
>
> ✓ his explanation of what it means to be a contender
>
> ✓ how he handles his boxers in training and during fights
>
> ✓ what he advises Spoon and Alfred to do with their lives

6. Alfred goes up the stairs to the gym and down the stairs to the clubroom. What other contrasts do you see between the gym and the clubroom?
7. **Literary Concept: Characterization** Which characters in the novel do you find believable and which do you not? Explain why.
8. **Making Connections** After finishing school, Alfred plans to work in a recreation center for African-American youths. How would you describe the effects that positive role models can have on the lives of young people? Use examples from your experiences and your reading to explain your ideas.

Writing Prompt

Write a **sports column** for a Harlem newspaper describing Alfred's bout with Elston Hubbard. Capture the drama of the third round, the emotions of the crowd, and the significance of the fight.

The Seventh Round

Discussion Starters

1. Describe your impressions of the speaker of this poem or draw a picture to show them.
2. What do you predict will happen to the speaker, and why?
3. Why do you think the speaker describes the mezzanine—the area around the ring where the crowd sits—as "dazzling dim" ?
4. How would you compare the speaker's attitude in the ring with Alfred's?

Writing Prompt

Write a **poem** from Alfred's perspective describing his thoughts and feelings during the final round against Elston Hubbard. Pattern the form of your poem on Merrill's "The Seventh Round."

Fury

Discussion Starters

1. How did you react to the ending of this story?
2. How would you account for the way Randy changes?
3. Explain whether or not Harlow is justified in tricking and manipulating his nephew Randy.
4. Who do you think has a brighter future, Randy or Alfred? Explain the reasons for your opinion.

Writing Prompt

Write an **outline** for a short story about a character who changes as a result of getting involved in a sport or a challenging activity.

BEFORE READING

You might want to distribute

 p. 27

AFTER READING

from The Story of My Life

Discussion Starters

1. What words do you think best describe Helen Keller?
2. In this excerpt from her autobiography, Helen Keller describes how she learned that everything has a name. How would you compare this process with the way that children who are not deaf and blind learn the same thing?
3. Imagine that Helen Keller had never met Miss Anne Sullivan. How do you think Helen's life might have been different?
4. How would you compare Anne Sullivan's relationship with Helen and Mr. Donatelli's relationship with Alfred? Support your views with details from the autobiography and the novel.

Writing Prompt

Think about someone who has had an important influence on your life. Write a **personal narrative** describing how this person influenced you.

A Crown of Wild Olive

Discussion Starters

1. What thoughts came to mind as you finished reading this story?

2. Whom would you rather have for a friend, Amyntas or Leon? Give reasons for your choice.

3. Near the end of the story, Amyntas realizes that he and Leon have exchanged "gifts of a sort." How would you explain what he means?

4. How would you explain why Amyntas and Leon, who come from warring cities with opposite values, become friends?

5. Who do you think is the better runner? Support your opinion with evidence from the story.

6. Athletic competition is an important value to Amyntas and Leon in this story and to Alfred in *The Contender*. In which of the three athletes does athletic competition bring out the best qualities? Support your choice with evidence.

7. How would you compare Amyntas's attitude toward the Olympic Games with that of a contemporary Olympic athlete?

Writing Prompt

When parting from his friend, Leon says, "The Gods be with you, Amyntas, and grant that we never meet again." Imagine that they do meet again, and then write a **sequel** to show what happens.

The Rights to the Streets of Memphis

Discussion Starters

1. Which part of the selection made the deepest impression on you? In your notebook, jot down your reaction at that point.
2. How do you think Richard's life might change as a result of his winning the fight?
3. How would you evaluate Mrs. Wright's treatment of her son?

> **CONSIDER**
> ✓ the neighborhood the family lives in
> ✓ her response to Richard after he is robbed the first time
> ✓ her response the second time he is robbed
> ✓ what Richard's life might be like if he doesn't learn to fight back

4. Whom do you admire more as a parent, and why—Richard's mother or Alfred's Aunt Pearl?

Writing Prompt

Imagine that Richard lost the fight and the grocery money. Write an alternative **story ending** describing the consequences.

Joan Benoit: 1984 U.S. Olympic Marathon Gold Medalist

Discussion Starters

1. What words describe your impressions of Joan Benoit?
2. Imagine that you are a reporter interviewing Joan Benoit after her winning performance. You ask her to identify the qualities that make her a winner. How do you think she might respond?
3. How would you compare Joan Benoit and Alfred as competitors?

Writing Prompt

You are a writer for a public relations firm covering the 1984 Olympics. Write a **character sketch** of Benoit for a souvenir program.

You might want to distribute
 p. 29

AFTER READING

Muhammad Ali

Discussion Starters

1. What are your thoughts about Muhammad Ali?
2. What do you consider Ali's greatest accomplishment? Explain why you think as you do.
3. How would you describe the qualities that made Muhammad Ali a hero to millions of people?
4. How would you compare Ali with your favorite sports hero?

Writing Prompt

Boxing is a violent sport, but neither Alfred Brooks in Lipsyte's novel nor Muhammad Ali in Littlefield's biography are brutal people outside the ring. Write an imaginary **dialogue** in which Alfred, *The Contender*, and Muhammad Ali, the former champion, discuss their views of boxing.

To the Field Goal Kicker in a Slump

AFTER READING

Discussion Starters

1. What words from this poem linger in your mind?
2. If you were in the kicker's place, how do you think you might have responded to the speaker?

> **CONSIDER**
> ✓ whether or not the speaker understands the kicker's frustration
> ✓ the comparison between writing and place kicking

3. Which character or characters in *The Contender* do you think would best relate to the kicker's feelings? Explain the reasons for your choice.
4. Losing or failing is a part of every sport, just as winning is. What important lessons do you think someone can learn from failing under pressure?

Writing Prompt

Write a **letter** that you might send to the kicker or to another athlete frustrated by failure.

These pages for the students give background, explain references, define vocabulary words, and help students connect their world with the world that Lipsyte creates in *The Contender*. You can reproduce these pages and allow students to read them before or while they read the works in *Literature Connections*.

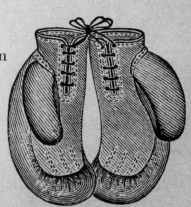

Table of Contents

The Contender

BACKGROUND

Separate or Integrate?

During the 1960s, the time period in which *The Contender* is set, many African Americans were torn between two social movements. On the one hand, the civil rights movement worked to end discrimination and segregation. Leaders in the movement sought integration in schools and housing and worked to elect African Americans to public office through

the extension of voting rights and registration. On the other hand, nationalist groups urged blacks to remain separate from whites, to start black businesses, and to form their own political unit. Among the chief black nationalist groups were the Black Muslims, who urged the creation of an all-black nation within the United States. One of the leading spokesmen of the Black Muslims during the 1960s was Malcolm X, who lived in New York City.

Weighing In and Fighting

In the sport of boxing, the fighters compete in divisions or classes based on their weight. For *amateurs,* those who may not accept money for boxing, there are 12 weight classes, shown in the table. For professionals, also called prizefighters because they fight for prize money, there are even more classes.

U.S. Amateur Weight Classes			
Class	**Pounds**	**Class**	**Pounds**
Super Heavyweight	Over 201	Heavyweight	179–201
Light Heavyweight	166–178	Middleweight	157–165
Light Middleweight	148–156	Welterweight	140–147
Light Welterweight	133–139	Lightweight	126–132
Featherweight	120–125	Bantamweight	113–119
Flyweight	107–112	Light Flyweight	Under 107

Boxing Greats

In *The Contender* a few actual boxing champions are mentioned as having visited Mr. Donatelli's ring: Joe Louis, Sugar Ray Robinson, and Cassius Clay, all African Americans.

- Joe Louis was the heavyweight champion of the world from 1937 to 1949, the longest reign of any boxer. Considered one of the greatest boxers of all time, Louis was known for his fast combinations of punches inside the ring and for being a gentleman outside the ring. He inspired tremendous pride among African Americans when he won the heavyweight championship from James J. Braddock in 1937, the first time an African American had held the title in twenty-two years.

- Sugar Ray Robinson was welterweight champion from 1946 to 1951 and won the middleweight championship five times. His nickname came from a sportswriter who described him as a "sweet as sugar" fighter.

- Cassius Clay, better known as Muhammad Ali, was a heavyweight champion in the 1960s and 1970s. A colorful and controversial figure, Ali adopted the Black Muslim religion and refused to be drafted during the Vietnam War. Known for his incredible speed and agility, Ali is considered by many to be the greatest boxer of all time.

VOCABULARY

Chapters 6, 7

Boxing Terms

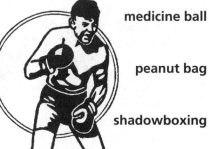

footwork	the way in which a boxer maneuvers his feet
hook	a short, swinging blow delivered with a crooked arm
medicine ball	a heavy, stuffed ball used in exercises to strengthen a boxer's stomach muscles
peanut bag	another word for a speed bag, or small punching bag
shadowboxing	practice boxing against an imaginary opponent
spar	to box in a practice match against a real opponent
stick	to flick out quick blows

Looking in the Mirror

As Alfred makes changes in his life, his self-image changes. And as he views himself differently, others tend to view him differently too. How does a person's self-image develop? What experiences help produce a positive self-image? A major influence on a person's self-image is the way that others view and treat that person from early on in life—the kind of mirror parents, teachers, other adults, and peers hold up to a person. If others view and treat a person positively, the person is more likely to view himself or herself positively. Another factor in the development of a positive self-image is the experience of attaining competence in some area—whether in school, sports, a hobby, or work. Especially during adolescence and young adulthood, many people struggle to resolve conflicts about self-image.

Behind Every Boxer

Behind every successful boxer is a trainer, like Mr. Donatelli in *The Contender*. Boxing trainers perform a variety of tasks and play multiple roles. They oversee a boxer's physical conditioning—running, exercising, sparring, and diet; they size up opponents and develop strategies for winning bouts; they advise and motivate a boxer in the corner between rounds; and they stop bouts before their boxer gets seriously hurt. A trainer acts as a father, a motivator, a mentor. The trainer has to know how to bring out the best in an individual fighter. To motivate their boxer in the ring, trainers employ a variety of methods, from begging to yelling to hitting. Angelo Dundee, who trained such champion boxers as Muhammad Ali and Sugar Ray Leonard, has said: "You can't be an even-keel kind of guy. You gotta create things that are gonna help that fighter. And if it means gruffness and it means pushing him and it means trying to put the bull on him, you gotta do it. Because the end result is you want to get that fighter juiced to try to win the fight." To spur Sugar Ray Leonard on to victory in a 1981 welterweight bout with Thomas Hearns, Dundee shouted into Leonard's ear after the twelfth round, "You've got nine minutes. You're blowing it. You're blowing it. This is what separates the men from the boys. You're blowing it." Leonard knocked out Hearns in the fourteenth round.

Chapters 10–20

SECTION 2

Boxing Terms

break lean to pull out of a clinch, or hold, and move completely away from an opponent

clinch the act of holding an opponent's body with one or both arms to prevent him from punching

combination two or more fast punches in a row

cross a blow thrown across the body at shoulder level

jab a quick blow made by extending an arm straight from the shoulder

slip to move one's head aside quickly to avoid a blow, letting the opponent's fist slip over one's shoulder

stick and run to flick out repeated jabs and dance out of reach

uppercut a swinging blow directed upward, such as to an opponent's chin

Chapter 16

Death and Injury in the Ring

After knocking out Griffin, Alfred worries about the possibility of killing an opponent in the ring. The risk of dying in a boxing ring is a very real one. According to a study in 1980, boxing is the most deadly of all contact sports, with an average of 21 deaths per year among 5,500 boxers in a nine-year period. Short of death, boxers face the risk of serious brain or eye damage. Some former boxers suffer from a condition known as punch-drunkenness, which is characterized by an unsteady gait, hand tremors, and slurred speech. Public attention focused on the dangers of boxing when South Korean fighter Duk Koo Kim died after a nationally televised bout with Ray "Boom Boom" Mancini in 1982.

Chapter 10

Early to Bed, Early to Rise

The training schedule that Alfred follows accurately reflects a boxer's typical regimen. Boxers spend several hours a day in training. They run to increase their endurance and stamina. They skip rope and do pushups, situps, and other conditioning exercises. They practice boxing skills by working out on punching bags and by boxing with sparring partners. Their diet, which consists of nutritious, lowfat foods, is carefully controlled to keep their weight within the narrow range for their weight division. Rocky Marciano, the world heavyweight champion from 1952 to 1956, became legendary for his strict training regimen. Before a championship fight, he would seclude himself for three or more months at a training camp in the Catskill Mountains, away from his family and all other distractions. He would devote himself exclusively to conditioning and training. Marciano won all 49 of his professional fights.

from The Story of My Life

BY HELEN KELLER

After the Breakthrough

After she grasped the meaning of the manual alphabet that Anne Sullivan was trying to teach her, Helen Keller progressed rapidly. Within three years, she had learned to read and write in Braille. Anne Sullivan stayed with Keller for her entire life. With Sullivan's help, Keller graduated from Radcliffe College with honors. She wrote many books and articles and worked tirelessly for the blind and the deaf-blind. She traveled the world, lecturing and raising funds for their behalf. The story of Keller's life has been told in the motion picture *Helen Keller in Her Story.* The play *The Miracle Worker,* which has been adapted into a film, depicts Sullivan's initial breakthrough with Keller.

Teacher with a Capital T

Anne Sullivan had firsthand experience with the difficulties of the blind. An orphan, Sullivan herself had vision problems as a child, and she had graduated from the Perkins Institution for the Blind in Boston. At Perkins she became acquainted with Laura Bridgman, the first deaf-blind person successfully educated in the United States. Surgery restored most of Sullivan's vision before she became Helen Keller's teacher. Although Sullivan was married for a time, she always remained with Keller, helping her write her books and traveling with her on lecture tours. Keller referred to her as *Teacher* with a capital T in her later correspondence.

The Inventor of the Telephone? Yes!

Alexander Graham Bell, who helped the Kellers find a teacher for Helen and who later became her friend, is remembered as the inventor of the telephone. Less well-known is Bell's lifelong work on behalf of the deaf. His mother and his wife were both deaf, and his father taught deaf-mutes to speak. Bell helped establish a laboratory to conduct research and develop inventions for the deaf, and he devoted time and money to finding ways to help the deaf learn to speak. He once spelled the following message into Helen's hand:

> **One would think I had never done anything worthwhile but the telephone. That is because it is a money-making invention. It is a pity so many people make money the criterion of success. I wish my experiences had resulted in enabling the deaf to speak with less difficulty. That would have made me truly happy.**

LITERARY CONCEPT

Simile

Helen Keller's writing is known for its literary qualities, including the use of figurative language. A *simile* is a figure of speech that states a comparison, using the word *like* or *as.* In the following simile, Keller compares her uneducated self to a ship in a dense fog:

> **Have you ever been at sea in a dense fog, when it seemed as if a tangible white darkness shut you in, and the great ship, tense and anxious, groped her way toward shore with plummet and sounding-line, and you waited with beating heart for something to happen? <u>I was like that ship before my education began</u>, only I was without compass or sounding-line and had no way of knowing how near the harbor was.**

A Crown of Wild Olive

BY ROSEMARY SUTCLIFF

Sparta and Athens at War

"A Crown of Wild Olive" is set during the time of a "long and weary war" between ancient Sparta and Athens—the Peloponnesian War, which lasted from 431 to 404 B.C. At that time, Greece was composed of small city-states, consisting of a central city and surrounding villages and farms. The Peloponnesian War grew out of a rivalry between Sparta, which had a strong military, and Athens, which had the greatest sea power. The war, which ended in Sparta's victory, led to the decline of the city-states of ancient Greece.

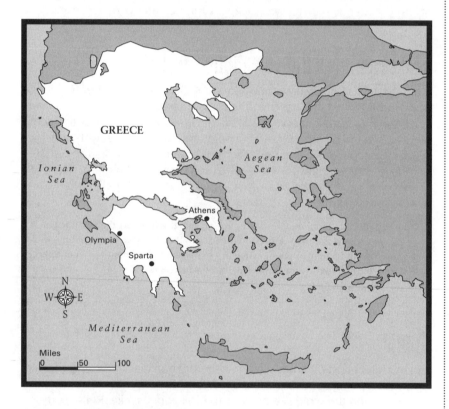

The Lean, Mean Spartans

The word *Spartan* is synonymous with self-discipline and a lack of luxury. In ancient times, the Spartan way of life was unusually harsh. A Spartan male was taken from his mother at age seven and placed in a military camp. At the camp, the boys slept on beds made of reeds and were allowed only one garment a year. Their food was sparse and tasteless, and they were taught to endure cold, hunger, pain, and tiredness without complaining.

The Liberal Athenians

In comparison to the Spartans, the Athenians had a liberal culture. They highly valued literature, art, and their democratic form of government. Athenian boys were expected to develop both their minds and their bodies. Until they were about 16 years old, Athenian boys studied reading, writing, arithmetic, music, dancing, and gymnastics. Then they were trained to become citizen-soldiers in government-sponsored schools that focused on sports and military art.

Let the Games Begin

Athletic competition was a basic part of ancient Greek religious festivals. The Greeks believed the contests pleased the spirits of the dead. The ancient Olympic Games, held every four years like many other festivals, honored the king of the Greek gods, Zeus. The first recorded Olympics took place in 776 B.C. in Olympia, with a 200-yard footrace the only athletic event. Over the years, longer races and other events were added, such as wrestling, the pentathlon (5 track and field events, usually sprinting, hurdling, long jumping, and discus and javelin throwing), boxing, and chariot racing.

Muhammad Ali

BY BILL LITTLEFIELD

The Silver-Tongued Ali

Muhammad Ali was a sportswriter's dream—he spouted off more quotable lines than any other sports figure before or since. Here are a few of Ali's quotable quotes.

Before his fight with Archie Moore—
When you come to the fight, don't block the aisle and don't block the door. You will all go home after round four.

Before his first fight with Sonny Liston—
I predict that he will go in eight to prove that I'm great; and if he wants to go to heaven, I'll get him in seven. He'll be in a worser fix if I cut it to six. And if he keeps talking jive, I'll cut it to five. . . . And if that don't do, I'll cut it to two. And if he run, he'll go in one.

Before his fight with George Foreman—
Float like a butterfly, sting like a bee.
His hands can't hit what his eyes can't see
Now you see me, now you don't
George thinks he will, but I know he won't.
(But what Ali actually used in the fight was a strategy he later called rope-a-dope, in which he leaned against the ropes and let his opponent wear himself out, throwing ineffective punches.)

On his Muslim faith—
Other churches preach pie in the sky when you die. We want something sound while we're around on the ground.

On his importance to boxing—
When I'm gone, boxing be nothing again. The fans with the cigars and the hats turned down will be there, but no more housewives and little men on the street and foreign presidents. I was the onliest boxer in history people asked questions like a senator.

Being a Muslim

Belief in the religion called Islam was and is an integral part of Muhammad Ali's life. Muslims believe that there is one God, called Allah, who created everything and will reward good and punish evil at the Last Judgment. According to Muslims, Allah's words have been revealed to people through a number of prophets, including Moses, Jesus, and Muhammad. A Muslim believer practices what are called the Five Pillars of Islam: (1) belief in one God, Allah, (2) prayer five times a day, (3) fasting during the month of Ramadan, (4) giving to the poor, and (5) performing a pilgrimage to Mecca once in a person's lifetime. Muslims are taught to refrain from drinking, gambling, and other vices.

Out of the Ring

Like many boxers before and since, Ali at first had a difficult time adjusting to life after boxing. But in time he came to terms with his retirement and with his physical impairments. Of his problems due to Parkinson's syndrome, Ali has said:

> So maybe this problem I have is God's way of reminding me and everyone else about what's important. I accept it as God's will. And I know that God never gives anyone a burden that's too heavy for them to carry.

Ali travels extensively, as part of business promotions and in support of various social causes. On occasion he has used his fame in political situations. For example, in 1990 he helped secure the release of 15 American hostages in Iraq. Of his life in retirement from boxing, Ali has said:

> Now my life is really starting. Fighting injustice, fighting racism, fighting crime, fighting illiteracy, fighting poverty, using this face the world knows so well, and going out and fighting for truth and different causes.
>
> Talking about boxing bores me now. Boxing was just to introduce me to the world. People today, they want me to talk like I used to. 'I'm the greatest! I'm the prettiest! I'm this, and I'm that!' But I don't want to do that no more. There's bigger work I got to do. . . . I want to live a good life, serve God, help everybody I can.

Glossary

Section 1: Chapters 1-9

bunion (bŭn'yən): *n.* a painful swelling on the big toe *p. 39*

cakewalk (kāk'wôk'): *v.* to perform a strutting dance *p. 66*

contender* (kən-tĕn'dər): *n.* one who competes, as in a sport *p. 25*

dog (dôg): *n. slang:* cowardice *p. 59*

junkie (jŭng'kē): *n.* a drug addict *p. 18*

lapse* (lăps): *v.* to pass slowly and smoothly; slip *p. 32*

liniment (lĭn'ə-mənt): *n.* an ointment rubbed into the skin to soothe pain or relieve stiffness *p. 20*

listlessness* (lĭst'lĭs-nĕs): *n.* a lack of energy *p. 27*

lope* (lōp): *v.* to walk or run with a steady, easy gait *p. 31*

murky* (mûr'kē): *adj.* dim *p. 20*

muted* (myo͞o'tĭd): *adj.* muffled *p. 17*

nationalist* (năsh'ə-nə-lĭzt'): *adj.* devoted to the interests of a particular nation or people *p. 27*

preliminary* (prĭ-lĭm'ə-nĕr'ē): *adj.* before the main event *p. 54*

quivering* (kwĭv-ər-ĭng): *adj.* trembling **quiver** *v.* *p. 20*

satchel (săch'əl): *n.* a small bag, often with shoulder straps *p. 47*

scowl* (skoul): *v.* to frown in disapproval *p. 30*

serenely* (sə-rēn'lē): *adv.* calmly *p. 27*

shambling* (shăm'blĭng): *adj.* shuffling **shamble** *v.* *p. 4*

sophisticated* (sə-fĭs'tĭ-kā'tĭd): *adj.* worldly and refined *p. 30*

stoop (sto͞op): *n.* a small set of stairs leading to the entrance of a house or apartment building *p. 3*

suave* (swäv): *adj.* smooth and refined in manner *p. 30*

swagger* (swăg'ər): *v.* to strut *p. 5*

synagogue* (sĭn'ə-gŏg'): *n.* a Jewish place of worship *p. 5*

Tom (tŏm): *v. slang:* to act meek and inferior in order to please whites *p. 27*

valise (və-lēs'): *n.* a small piece of hand luggage *p. 48*

Section 2: Chapters 10-20

biceps* (bī'sĕps): *n.* the front upper arm muscle *p. 107*

boardwalk (bôrd'wôk'): *n.* a promenade, usually made of planks, along a waterfront *p. 90*

mimeographed (mĭm'ē-ə-grăfd'): *adj.* copied on a mimeograph machine, which uses a stencil fitted around an inked drum **mimeograph** *v.* *p. 144*

pummel* (pŭm'əl): *v.* to beat with the fists *p. 149*

silhouetted* (sĭl'o͞o-ĕt'ĭd): *adj.* appearing as a dark outline against a light background **silhouette** *v.* *p. 97*

vault* (vôlt): *v.* to jump *p. 91*

PARTIAL PRONUNCIATION KEY

ă	at, gas	îr	dear, here	th	thing, with
ā	ape, day	ng	sing, anger	th	then, other
ä	father, barn	ŏ	odd, not	ŭ	up, nut
âr	fair, dare	ō	open, road, grow	ûr	fur, earn, bird, worm
ĕ	egg, ten	ô	awful, bought, horse	zh	treasure, garage
ē	evil, see, meal	oi	coin, boy	ə	awake, even, pencil,
hw	white, everywhere	o͝o	look, full		pilot, focus
ĭ	inch, fit	o͞o	root, glue, through	ər	perform, letter
ī	idle, my, tried	ou	out, cow		

SOUNDS IN FOREIGN WORDS

kh	*German* ich, auch; *Scottish* loch	œ	*French* feu, cœur; *German* schön	ü	*French* utile, rue; *German* grün
n	*French* entre, bon, fin				

---

* The words followed by asterisks are useful words that you might add to your vocabulary.

Making Inferences

As you read a novel such as *The Contender*, you make inferences, or logical guesses, about why events happen or why characters act as they do. You base these inferences on the evidence you find in the story as well as on your own experiences. On the chart below, write down an inference in the column on the right to explain each event listed in the column on the left. The first one is done for you.

What happens	Why?
Alfred refuses to take part in an attempt to rob his employer's store despite peer pressure to do so.	Perhaps largely because of the influence of Aunt Pearl, a religious and loving caretaker, Alfred has a strong sense of right and wrong. He wants to do right, and he feels loyal to people who have been kind to him, such as Mr. Epstein.
Alfred enters Donatelli's gym and tells him he wants to be a fighter.	
Donatelli describes the difficulties that boxing involves and advises Alfred not to take up the sport.	
Despite feeling uncertain about his direction in life, Alfred starts running in the mornings and trains at the gym to become a boxer.	
Donatelli stops Willie Streeter's fight in Madison Square Garden.	
Despite threats, Alfred refuses to help Major rob Mr. Epstein's store, and he later tells Aunt Pearl he's decided to become a boxer.	

Strategic Reading ②

Identifying Influences on a Character

As you read a novel, you may come across one or more characters who change greatly. By the end of *The Contender*, for example, Alfred has found a new direction for his life. He has decided to finish school and then work in a recreation center for youth. Think about what motivates Alfred to reach this decision. Then, on the chart below, describe what Alfred learns from each of the influences listed. The first one is done for you.

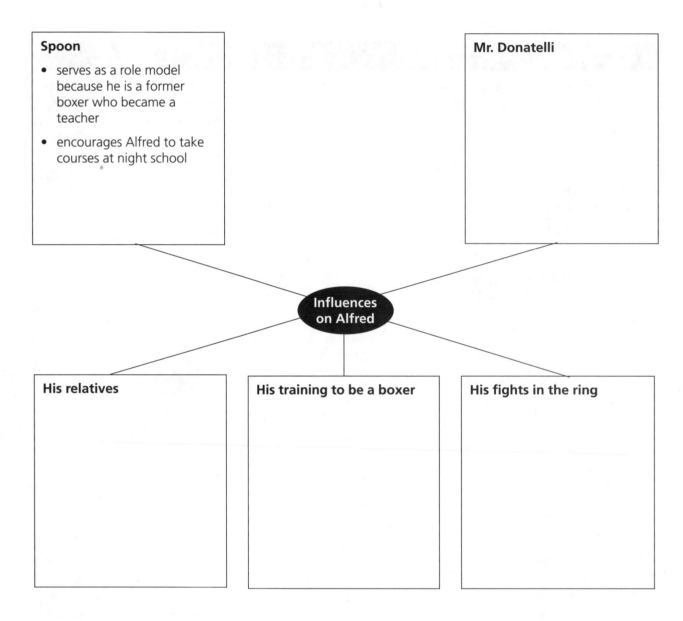

Spoon

• serves as a role model because he is a former boxer who became a teacher

• encourages Alfred to take courses at night school

Mr. Donatelli

Influences on Alfred

His relatives

His training to be a boxer

His fights in the ring

Literary Concept (1)

THEME

A **theme** is a message about life or human nature that is conveyed by a literary work. A work may have more than one theme, and in many cases readers must infer the writer's messages and may state them in different ways. On the chart below are statements of some of the themes that *The Contender* might convey. For each statement, write down one or more events in the novel that suggest the theme to you. Then write down one or more events from real life that convey the same theme.

Statements of theme	Events from the novel	Events from real life
• It's the effort and struggle that make a person, not winning or success.		
• It takes courage, discipline, hard work, and inner strength to change one's life.		
• Each person must try to find out what he or she is capable of achieving.		
• Young people need friends and/or role models to help and guide them.		

Literary Concept 2

CHARACTERIZATION

Characterization is the way writers make characters seem real. There are four basic techniques that writers use to create and develop characters:

• describing the character's appearance

• presenting the character's thoughts, words, and actions

• showing others' responses to the character

• directly commenting on the character's nature

Fill in the chart below to see how Lipsyte uses some or all of these techniques to create the characters listed. After you have completed the chart, circle the name of the technique that you think worked especially well in making the characters come alive.

Character	Appearance	Thoughts, Words, and Actions	Others' Responses	Author's Comments
Alfred	average height, thin, with big hands	Stands up to Major, refusing to go along with a robbery	Jeff says Alfred has changed from being negative and directionless	
Aunt Pearl				
Major				
Donatelli				
Spoon				
James				

Conflict is a struggle between opposing forces. In an **external conflict,** a character struggles against another character or against some outside force. **Internal conflict,** on the other hand, is a struggle within a character. In *The Contender*, Alfred Brooks experiences both external and internal conflicts as he struggles to find direction in his life. The chart below will help you explore some of these conflicts. In each of the rectangles, describe the conflict listed, classify it as external or internal, and write down the outcome.

Force vs. Opposing force	Description of conflict	Type	Outcome
Alfred vs. James			

Force vs. Opposing force	Description of conflict	Type	Outcome
Alfred vs. Major			

Force vs. Opposing force	Description of conflict	Type	Outcome
Black nationalists vs. Reverend Price			

Force vs. Opposing force	Description of conflict	Type	Outcome
Alfred's need to be "somebody" vs. his growing dislike for boxing			

Name

Review the asterisked words from the Glossary. Then complete the activities below.

A. Use the clues to fill in the crossword puzzle.

Clues

Down

1. shake

2. refined

3. gloomy and dim

4. glare

7. punch

Across

5. leap

6. stride

8. arm muscles

B. In each set of words below, circle the word that does not belong with the others.

1. swagger	strut	stride	creep
2. quiet	serene	troubled	tranquil
3. gracious	suave	coarse	polished
4. energetic	listless	sluggish	lazy
5. preliminary	final	following	concluding

Beyond the Literature
SYNTHESIZING IDEAS

Culminating Writing Assignments

EXPLORATORY WRITING

1. Do you think participation in sports helps develop character? Write an **opinion column** for your school newspaper in which you discuss your opinion on the value of sports in students' lives. Cite examples from *The Contender* to support your views.

2. Given the direction that Alfred is taking at the end of the novel, what do you imagine him doing in ten years? Write an **epilogue** to the story, telling what Alfred's life is like when he is in his late twenties.

3. Write an **essay** comparing *The Contender* to another young adult novel that centers on sports. As a focus for your essay, you might choose from among the following topics:
   - the characterizations of the novels
   - how believable the characters are
   - how the main character changes from participating in a sport

RESEARCH

1. Lipsyte wrote *The Contender* during the height of the black nationalist movement of the 1960s. Research this movement, exploring its leaders, its goals, and its results. Write a **research report** to present your findings.

2. Research the life and career of one of the famous boxers mentioned in the novel—Joe Louis, Sugar Ray Robinson, or Cassius Clay—or a more recent champion. Find out what the champion's life was like after leaving boxing. Write a brief **biography** of the boxer.

LITERARY ANALYSIS

1. State a theme of the novel in your own words, or choose one of the statements of theme that you explored while completing the **Literary Concept 1** worksheet. Then write a **critical essay** in which you explain how the novel conveys the theme you have chosen. Use specific scenes and details from the novel to demonstrate the theme.

2. A **symbol** is a person, a place, an object, or an action that stands for something beyond itself. Think of places that are important to the characterization of this novel, such as the clubroom, Mr. Donatelli's gym, and the cave in the park. Then write a **review** explaining what you think these places might symbolize in the novel.

3. According to critic Nat Hentoff, "*The Contender* . . . fails as believable fiction." Write an **opinion essay** stating whether or not you agree with this statement, supporting your views with evidence from the novel.

Multimodal Activities

From Page to Stage

Have students choose a key scene from the novel and prepare and present a **dramatization** of it for the class. Some scenes you might suggest to students include

- when Alfred walks into the gym for the first time and meets Mr. Donatelli (Chapters 2 and 3)
- when Mr. Donatelli advises Alfred to give up boxing (Chapter 18)
- when Alfred finds James hiding in the cave in the park (Chapter 20)

Pumping Up

Suggest that students create a National Fitness Week **poster** promoting the benefits of athletics for teenagers. You might display these posters in the classroom or a school corridor.

Before and After

Suggest that students draw or paint a **two-panel portrait** of Alfred Brooks, depicting him before and after taking up boxing. Tell students to include illustrations of things that relate to important events in each of these stages of his life. Students might give their portrait a title and display it in class.

Make the Scene

Have students use details from the novel to create a **diorama** of Donatelli's gym. They might include clay figures of boxers working out in the gym and of Bud and Mr. Donatelli coaching them.

Tell It to the Judge

Challenge students to imagine themselves as a public defender for James who is on trial for attempting to rob Epstein's grocery store. Have them prepare and present a **summation,** a closing argument that summarizes the important points of the case and recommends a course of action.

Drum Up Business

Have students imagine that they run a training gym or health club. Students should design an **advertisement** for a newspaper or a magazine to promote business. The advertisement should feature illustrations, motivational sayings, and a catchy slogan.

Act It Out

Tell students to choose an athlete that they admire and research his or her life. Then have students present an **impersonation** of the athlete, telling the class what he or she has learned from playing a particular sport.

Just Say Yes

Suggest that students create a **handout** for high school dropouts, urging them to return to school. The handout should mention the benefits of obtaining a high school diploma and the drawbacks of not having one. Students might include some examples from the novel to develop their argument.

Going Up the Stairs

Before writing *The Contender*, Robert Lipsyte asked himself this question: "What are the moments in life that are equivalent to 'going up the stairs?' " Suggest that a group of students write a **skit** about a life experience that they consider similar to "going up the stairs." Have students perform the skit for the class.

Talk About It

Have students view the film *Hoop Dreams*, listed in the Additional Resources on page 49. Then have them hold a **panel discussion** on the benefits and drawbacks of a strong emphasis on sports for disadvantaged youth. Encourage students to compare Alfred's situation with the situations of the youths presented in the film.

Breaking a Sweat

Overview:

This project involves making a videotaped documentary about the training of student athletes. The students will work collaboratively to interview student athletes and videotape them in action. The purpose of this activity is to compare the training regimens of fellow students with Alfred's in *The Contender*.

Cross-Curricular Connections: Physical Education, Health, Film

Suggested Procedure:

1. Divide students into small groups. Have each group choose a sport in which students at your school participate, such as gymnastics, soccer, or basketball. Each group should choose a different sport. Explain to students that they will interview and videotape fellow students who participate in the sport. (Set a reasonable time limit for the length of the completed videotapes.)

2. Have each group brainstorm a list of questions about the training regimen of athletes in the chosen sport. Students should consider both exercises and diet. You might suggest sample questions to get students started, such as

- What stretching exercises do you do before a workout?
- What do you do to improve your skills?
- How do you increase your endurance?
- What are the best foods for an athlete in training?

3. Tell each group to find several students who are willing to be interviewed and filmed for the project. Have students conduct and videotape the interviews and also film the athletes in action.

4. Students might also interview the coach of the sport, asking about training procedures and recommended diet.

5. To complete the project, students should compare the training regimen of the athletes they've interviewed with the one that Alfred follows in the novel. Have students present their conclusions at the end of their videotape.

6. Allow the groups to show their videotapes. You might follow the viewings with a discussion of what students learned from the project and what questions it raised.

> **Teaching Tip**
>
> You might coordinate this project with a physical education or health teacher. The teacher might discuss with students the primary muscle groups used in different sports, the purposes of different types of exercises, and the importance of diet in an athlete's conditioning.

Doing it Your Way

Overview:

In *The Contender*, Mr. Donatelli has definite principles that guide him in managing the boxers he trains. In this project, students will work cooperatively to list the principles that they think a manager or coach should follow in running a sports team.

Cross-Curricular Connections: Physical Education, Social Studies

Suggested Procedure:

1. Have students imagine that they are the manager of a sports team, such as a little league baseball team, a gymnastics squad, or a school volley ball team. As managers, they are responsible for deciding how to run the team and for drawing up a list of *maxims*—or short statements of basic principles—to guide them in managing their athletes.

2. Have each student list five maxims that he or she thinks a manager should take to heart. In listing these maxims, students should consider not only the values that managers should try to instill in athletes but also nitty-gritty concerns, such as who gets to start for the team and who gets the most playing time.

3. Have students work in groups consisting of four or five members each. Group members should share their lists, identify the maxims they agree on, and debate the ones that stir controversy. As a group, they should try to come up with a list of ten maxims. (Note: In some groups, the members may have difficulty reaching a consensus because of basic differences in their guiding philosophies. You might allow these groups to present two or more lists that reflect the different philosophies.)

4. Have each group choose a spokesperson to present the list of maxims to the class. After each presentation, allow the rest of the class to discuss the group's choices. Finally, have students discuss how they imagine Mr. Donatelli would have responded to the maxims on the list.

Teaching Tip

You might broaden this assignment by having students interview coaches about their philosophy of managing a sports team or by having a coach speak to the class.

Suggestions for Assessment

Negotiated Rubrics

Negotiating rubrics for assessment with students allows them to know before they start an assignment what is required and how it will be judged, and gives them additional ownership of the final product. A popular method of negotiating rubrics is for the teacher and students individually to list the qualities that the final product should contain, then compare the teacher-generated list with the student-generated list and together decide on a compromise.

Portfolio Building

Remind students that they have many choices of types of assignments to select for their portfolios. Among these are the following:

- Culminating Writing Assignments (page 37)
- Writing Prompts, found in the Discussion Starters
- Multimodal Activities (page 38–39)
- Cross-Curricular Projects (pages 40–41)

Suggest that students use some of the following questions as criteria in selecting which pieces to include in their portfolios.

- Which shows my clearest thinking about the literature?
- Which is or could become most complete?
- Which shows a type of work not presently included in my portfolio?
- Which am I proudest of?

Remind students to reflect on the pieces they choose and to attach a note explaining why they included each and how they would evaluate it.

For suggestions on how to assess portfolios, see **Teacher's Guide to Assessment and Portfolio Use.**

Writing Assessment

The following can be made into formal assignments for evaluation:

- Culminating Writing Assignments page 00
- a written analysis of the Critic's Corner literary criticism
- fully developed Writing Prompts from the Discussion Starters

For suggestions about assessing specific kinds of writing, see **The Guide to Writing Assessment** *in the* **Formal Assessment Booklet.**

Test

The test on pages 43–44 consists of essay and short-answer questions. The answer key follows.

Alternative Assessment

For the kinds of authentic assessment found on many state and districtwide tests, see the **Alternative Assessment** booklet of **The Language of Literature.**

Test

Essay

Choose two of the following essay questions to answer on your own paper. (25 points each)

1. The young male characters in *The Contender*—Alfred, James, and Major— react differently to their situation in life. Describe their situation and the ways that each character reacts to it.

2. Mr. Donatelli obviously has strong beliefs about boxing and about life. How would you describe the main points of his belief system?

3. Do you think Alfred should quit boxing or continue in the ring? Explain your answer.

4. Describe the way that each of the following characters affects Alfred: Aunt Pearl, Uncle Wilson, James, Mr. Donatelli, and Spoon. Use details from the novel to fill in the chart before writing your essay.

Character	Effect on Alfred
Aunt Pearl	
Uncle Wilson	
James	
Mr. Donatelli	
Spoon	

5. Choose one of the following pairs to compare and contrast:

   a. Alfred in *The Contender* and Randy in "Fury"

   b. the neighborhoods of Harlem in *The Contender* and the neighborhood of Memphis in "The Rights to the Streets of Memphis"

   c. Mr. Donatelli in *The Contender* and Anne Sullivan in the excerpt from Helen Keller's autobiography

Short Answer

On your paper, write a short answer for each question below and give a reason for your answer. (5 points each)

1. Why do you think Donatelli tells Alfred that quitting before you really try is worse than never starting at all?

2. What is the greatest conflict or struggle that Alfred faces?

3. Do you consider Alfred a "contender"? Explain your answer.

4. How does Aunt Pearl show her love for Alfred?

5. How would you explain why Mr. Donatelli tells Spoon and Alfred to give up boxing?

6. What effect does boxing have on Alfred's self-image, and why?

7. Is Spoon a believable character? Give reasons for your opinion.

8. How would you explain why Alfred is able to overcome the obstacles in his life while James is not?

9. What do you think the cave might represent to Alfred and James?

10. Why is Alfred so sure he can help James at the end of the novel?

Essay

Answers to essay questions will vary, but ideas should be stated clearly and supported by details from the novel. Suggestions for points to look for are given below.

1. Students may note that the three young men live in an impoverished neighborhood, plagued by drug abuse and crime. As black men, they feel trapped by the lack of opportunity in a white man's world. Alfred and James both drop out of school. But while James falls into a life of drug abuse and crime, Alfred gets a job and looks for a way out of poverty by taking up boxing. Major becomes the leader of a neighborhood gang of thugs and tries to lure or intimidate Alfred and other youths into joining.

2. Students may say Mr. Donatelli believes that, in sports and in life, what matters is how much effort a person puts into it, not whether he or she is successful. He tells Alfred that it's the struggle that makes the man and that he must try his hardest once he starts something. Donatelli believes that people must control their fears and work hard to accomplish anything.

3. Some students may think Alfred should quit the ring for the following reasons: he doesn't like to hurt his opponents, he has good plans for his future, he's gotten everything he can get out of the sport, he doesn't have the killer instinct to become a champion, and sooner or later he will get badly hurt if he continues to box. Others may feel that Alfred should not give up on boxing while he's still successful at it. He did fight heroically against Elston Hubbard, a brutal fighter who had knocked out all his other opponents. They may think it simply takes time for a boxer to get used to having to hurt his opponent to win.

4. Students might list effects similar to the following:

   Aunt Pearl—makes Alfred feel loved, gives him some stability in life, helps him develop a sense of right and wrong

   Uncle Wilson—provides a role model of a successful black man, makes Alfred think about his life plans

   James—as a boyhood friend, gives Alfred companionship and support but also is responsible for trying to lead Alfred astray

   Mr. Donatelli—impresses Alfred with his philosophy of life, helps Alfred learn discipline and the importance of hard work, encourages Alfred to pursue his goals outside of boxing

   Spoon—serves as a positive role model for Alfred; gives Alfred the guidance, support, and encouragement he needs to change his life

5. **a.** Both Alfred and Randy Fuller find direction in life through boxing and the influence of caring adults. However, Alfred is quiet, sensible, and mild-mannered, while Randy Fuller is foolish and hot-tempered.

   b. Both neighborhoods are impoverished areas where stronger boys terrorize and beat up weaker ones. The streets are where youths have to prove themselves strong enough to survive.

c. Both Mr. Donatelli and Anne Sullivan are disciplined teachers who take a deeply personal interest in the young people they train. Mr. Donatelli helps Alfred to find a direction in life, and Anne Sullivan gives Helen the power of language.

Short Answer

Answers will vary but should reflect the following ideas.

1. Mr. Donatelli believes that you have to put your entire self into trying to accomplish something, rather than make half-hearted attempts. If Alfred doesn't really try, he'll never knows whether or not he has what it takes to succeed.

2. Some students may believe that Alfred's greatest struggle is overcoming the temptation to follow the same path that James did. Others may say that Alfred's greatest struggle is to overcome his own self-doubts, his fear of failing again.

3. Alfred never becomes recognized as a contender in the world of boxing, but he becomes a contender in life by learning to control his fear and to put his heart into accomplishing something. He learns that climbing is the true test of character.

4. Aunt Pearl provides a good home, she physically and verbally expresses her concern for Alfred, and she lets him pursue his own dreams.

5. Mr. Donatelli believes Spoon and Alfred have the talent to accomplish better things outside the ring than in the world of boxing.

6. Boxing bolsters Alfred's self-image because by learning its discipline he proves to himself that he can overcome great challenges if he tries.

7. Some students may think Spoon is a believable character because he is similar to other people who have overcome obstacles to achieve something and who work to help others do so. Other students may think that Spoon does not come across as believable because he seems completely good and understanding, as in his reaction to the student who pulls a knife on him.

8. Even though Alfred's parents are dead, he has a stable, loving home with his aunt. James, on the other hand, comes from an abusive home. Alfred's stable, supportive home helps give him the inner strength that James lacks.

9. To both Alfred and James, the cave represents a safe place, a refuge when life's problems get overwhelming.

10. Alfred is confident because he has learned that he has the heart and the will of a contender. The qualities he shows in his fight against Elston Hubbard he can draw upon to meet any challenge.

Selected Works by Robert Lipsyte
(FOR YOUNG ADULTS)

Assignment: Sports, Harper. 1970, revised edition, 1984.
This is a collection of twenty-four vignettes about sports.

One Fat Summer, 1977.
Fourteen-year-old Bobby Marks loses weight and changes his self-image.

Free to Be Muhammad Ali, 1978
A biography of the famous heavyweight boxing champion.

Summer Rules, 1981.
The sequel to *One Fat Summer,* continuing the story of Bobby Marks.

The Suimmerboy, 1982.
The third novel in the trilogy about Bobby Marks.

Jock and Jill, 1982.
The main characters in this novel are a high school baseball player and his girlfriend, who is a drug user.

The Brave, 1991.
In the sequel to *The Contender*, Albert Brooks, a police sergeant, helps a runaway Native American named Sonny Bear.

The Chemo Kid, 1992.
The story of a boy who battles cancer.

The Chief, 1993.
The sequel to *The Brave*, with Alfred as Sonny Bear's boxing trainer.

Arnold Schwarzenegger: Hercules in America, 1993.
A biography of the famous body builder and actor.

Jim Thorpe: Twentieth-Century Jock, 1993.
A biography of the Olympic track-and-field champion of the early 1900s.

Joe Louis: A Champ for all America, 1994.
A biography of the world heavyweight champion from 1937 to 1949.

Michael Jordan: Life above the Rim, 1994.
A biography of the famous Chicago Bulls basketball player.

(FOR ADULTS)

The Masculine Mystique, 1966.
A satire on the women's liberation movement.

Something Going (with Steve Cady), 1973.
A novel about the world of thoroughbred horse racing.

SportsWorld: An American Dreamland, 1975.
A collection of essays about the world of athletics.

Idols of the Game: A Sporting History of the American Century
(with Peter Levine), 1995.
Profiles of sixteen American sports champions, with discussions of how
their careers and lives reflect American culture.

FICTION

Bonham, Frank. *Durango Street.* Dutton, 1965. This novel depicts the
world of teenage gangs. **(easy)**

Childress, Alice. *A Hero Ain't Nothin' but a Sandwich.* Avon, 1973. In
this novel set in Harlem, a 13-year-old struggles to overcome a heroin
addiction. **(average)**

Myers, Walter Dean. *Hoops.* Delacorte Press, 1981. A teenaged basketball player from Harlem has a chance to impress college scouts if he
doesn't ruin the opportunity. **(average)**

Soto, Gary. *Baseball in April and Other Stories.* Harcourt, 1990. A collection of short stories about Latino youth growing up in California.
(average)

Soto, Gary. *Taking Sides.* Harcourt, 1991. A talented basketball player
must adjust to change after moving from an inner-city to a suburban
high school. **(easy)**

Spinelli, Jerry. *Maniac Magee.* Little, Brown, 1990. A mythical story
about an athletic boy who breaks the barriers between segregated
parts of a town. **(average)**

Voigt, Cynthia. *The Runner.* Atheneum, 1985. A 17-year-old cross-
country runner coaches a fellow student and in the process learns to
accept responsibility, overcome his prejudices, and free himself from his
authoritarian father. **(challenge)**

NONFICTION

Gunton, Sharon R., ed. "Robert Lipsyte." *Contemporary Literary
Criticism.* Vol. 21. Gale Research, 1982. A collection of excerpts from
critical reviews of Lipsyte's works.

Olendorf, Donna, ed. "Lipsyte, Robert (Michael) 1938-" *Something
About the Author.* Vol. 68. Gale Research, 1992. A biographical sketch
of Robert Lipsyte.

Senick, Gerard J., ed. "Robert Lipsyte." *Children's Literature Review.*
Vol. 23. Gale Research, 1991. A collection of excerpts from critical
reviews of Lipsyte's works as well as a commentary by the author about
sports.

MULTIMEDIA

Boxer. Video recording, Temple University, 1975. 15 minutes. A look at modern boxing in relation to its origins in ancient Greece and Rome. **(videocassette)**

Boxing's Greatest Knockouts & Highlights. Video recording, Simitar Entertainment, Karol Video, 1990. 30 minutes. Historic fights featuring Joe Frazier, Muhammad Ali, Sugar Ray Leonard, and Leon Spinks. **(videocassette)**

Herschel Walker's Fitness Challenge for Kids. Video recording, HPG Home Video, 40 minutes. Former football-great Herschel Walker counsels youngsters against the use of drugs and alcohol and promotes the value of exercise. **(videocassette)**

Hoop Dreams. Video recording, New Line Home Video, 1994. 169 minutes. An award-winning documentary about the actual lives of two Chicago youths who dream of playing basketball in the NBA. Rated PG-13. **(videocassette)**

Rocky. Video recording, United Artists/Intervision, 1976. 119 minutes. Starring Sylvester Stallone. This sentimental, but uplifting, film tells the story of a down-and-out boxer who gets a chance to fight for the championship. Rated PG. **(videocassette)**